The Daily Don

All the News that Fits into Tiny, Tiny Hands

JESSE DUQUETTE

Arcade Publishing · New York

Arcade Publishing books may be purchased in bulk at special discounts for sales promotion, corporate gifts, fund-raising, or educational purposes. Special editions can also be created to specifications. For details, contact the Special Sales Department, Arcade Publishing, 307 West 36th Street, 11th Floor, New York, NY 10018 or arcade@skyhorsepublishing.com.

Arcade Publishing® is a registered trademark of Skyhorse Publishing, Inc.®, a Delaware corporation.

Visit our website at www.arcadepub.com.

10 9 8 7 6 5 4 3 2 1

Library of Congress Cataloging-in-Publication Data is available on file.

Print ISBN: 978-1-948924-42-9
Ebook ISBN: 978-1-948924-43-6

Printed in the United States of America

FOREWORD BY JESSE DUQUETTE

1

THE FIRST WORST 100 DAYS

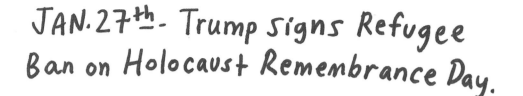

JAN. 27th - Trump signs Refugee
Ban on Holocaust Remembrance Day.

"I call him religious who understands
the suffering of others."

~ Mahatma Gandhi

Feb. 27th - Spicer cracks down on White House leaks, checks staff's cell phones for correspondence with reporters, which is immediately leaked.

"To the man who is afraid, everything rustles." ~ Sophocles

Mar. 4th- Without any evidence or proof, Trump accuses Obama of wiretapping his phones.

" I'm the most terrific liar you ever saw in your life." ~ J.D. Salinger

March 9ᵗʰ. Trump mulls cutting $6B from public housing to fund larger military.

"Every gun that is made, every warship launched... signifies a theft from those who hunger and are not fed, those who are cold and are not clothed."
~ Dwight D. Eisenhower

"Supposing is good, but finding out is better."
~ Mark Twain

Mar. 21st- Former Trump campaign manager
is revealed to have earned $10M a year to
help push Putin's interests throughout
Europe and U.S., a charge he denies.

"The louder he talked of his honor, the
faster we counted our spoons."
— Ralph Waldo Emerson

Mar. 23rd - In Time Magazine interview
Trump defends his most controversial
claims, from Obama wiretapping to Cruz's
father's connections to JFK assassination.

"I'm President and you're not."

"It must be wonderful to be seventeen
and to know everything."
— Arthur C. Clarke

Mar. 25th - Trump goes on 12th golfing trip
in 9 weeks at a cost of $3M to taxpayers/trip.

"Let people work hard and aspire to some
day be able to play golf."
        — Donald J. Trump

Mar. 28th - Trump signs executive order curbing enforcement of climate regulations, lifts ban on coal leasing on federal land.

April 6th - Nunes "temporarily" steps aside
from Russia investigation following numerous
ethics complaints.

"Subservience is degrading, even if
   you like it."
                    — Marty Rubin

April 11th~

"(Hitler) was not using the gas on his own people the same way that Assad is doing... he brought them into Holocaust centers."

"It is my task always to know, particularly when I don't."
— Gore Vidal

April 18th - Citing no evidence, Trump blames Obama for MS-13 gang forming in U.S.

"Everything you can imagine is real."
~Pablo Picasso

April 19th - 7 current and former U.S. officials confirm that a Russian gov't think tank controlled by Putin developed a plan to swing the 2016 election to Trump.

"No puppet. No puppet. You're the puppet!"
   -Donald J. Trump

April 22nd - Trump releases Earth Day statement touting his commitment to "keeping our air and water clean, to preserving our forests, lakes, and open spaces, and to protecting endangered species."

April 24th-

"Nothing saddens me more than seeing how
quickly the dog grows used to its leash."
~ Marty Rubin

2

IN WHICH BACKBONES ARE A LIBERAL HOAX, BELIEVE ME

May 1st - Trump calls Kim Jong Un a "really smart cookie", says he'd be "honored" to meet with him under the right circumstances.

"Standing each by his monster, they looked at each other, and smiled."   ~ E.M. Forster

- FREED 4* HOSTAGES FROM NORTH KOREA

- BRAGGED ABOUT T.V. RATINGS

- LIED ABOUT WHEN 2 OF THE HOSTAGES WERE CAPTURED

- USED OCCASION TO SAY "EVERYONE" THINKS HE SHOULD GET NOBEL PEACE PRIZE

* 1 HOSTAGE CAME BACK TORTURED AND BRAIN DAMAGED BY "REALLY EXCELLENT" KIM JONG-UN AND DIED A SHORT WHILE LATER

- FREED 11 HOSTAGES FROM NORTH KOREA

- DIDN'T DO ANY OF THAT OTHER DUMB SHIT

May 9th - Trump fires Comey amid FBI Director's investigation into collusion between Russia and Trump campaign.

"Like all bullies and marauders, he was a coward at heart."

~ L. Frank Baum

May 10th - Spicer responds to Comey firing by hiding in bushes, demanding darkness.

"Hide until everybody goes home. Hide until everybody forgets about you. Hide until everybody dies."
 — Yoko Ono

May 15th - WH officials say Trump revealed highly classified information to Russian foreign minister and ambassador during Oval Office meeting.

Sing for us, Comrade!

"And we are on the track of the guilty persons."
~ Alexandre Dumas

June 7th –

"What is the son but an extension of the
father?"   — Frank Herbert

"Things come apart so easily when they have been held together with lies."

— Dorothy Allison

June 28th - Time Magazine asks President who hates "fake news" to remove fake magazine covers from clubs.

"Confidence is the prize given to the mediocre."
~Robert Hughes

"The President in no way, form, or fashion has ever promoted or encouraged violence."

— Sarah Huckabee Sanders

"Guard against the impostures of pretended patriotism." — George Washington

July 9th - Trump says he and Putin discussed forming "impenetrable Cyber Security unit" to combat hacking and "many other negative things".

"It is stupidity rather than courage to refuse to recognize danger when it is close upon you."

— Sir Arthur Conan Doyle

July 11th - Trump Jr. tweets email exchange about meetings between himself and Russian lawyer that details Russian government's "support for Trump" and Trump Jr.'s eagerness to receive damaging info.

"I can handle things! I'm smart! Not like everybody says... like dumb... I'm smart and I want respect!"   — Fredo Corleone

"Remember, you are not dealing with creatures of logic but with creatures bristling with prejudice and motivated by pride and vanity."   - Dale Carnegie

July 20th - Ignoring Trump's threats, Special Counsel to examine President's finances.

" A guilty person sometimes has the luck to escape detection, but never to feel sure of it."
— Seneca

July 26th - Trump tweets that transgender individuals will not be allowed "to serve in any capacity in the U.S. military."

"Please try to remember that what they believe, as well as what they do and cause you to endure, does not testify to your inferiority but to their inhumanity and fear."
— James Baldwin

July 28th - Reince Priebus pushed out of WH Chief of Staff job over Scaramucci acrimony.

"The wild things roared their terrible roars and gnashed their terrible teeth and rolled their terrible eyes and showed their terrible claws but Max stepped into his private boat and waved goodbye."

—Maurice Sendak

3

A SEASON OF CHARLOTTESVILLE AND CHARLATANS

"Reality irritated him, frightened him, kept him in continual agitation, and, perhaps to justify his aversion for the actual, he always praised the past and what had never existed."

— Anton Chekhov

July 29th - Trump encourages police officers to "rough" up suspected criminals, describes cities as "bloodstained killing fields" overrun by undocumented immigrants.

"A violent order is disorder; and a great disorder is an order. These two things are one."

—Wallace Stevens

Aug. 2nd - In attempting to defend Trump's immigration efforts, WH aide Miller says Statue of Liberty poem has no significance.

WE SERVE WHITES only

JAN 20 MMXXI

"Me and the United States is dissociating our alliance as of right now, until the United States can find time to read its own textbooks a little."
— James Jones

"From one dog, all the dogs bark."
— Marty Rubin

Aug. 15th - During infrastructure speech
Trump defends symbols of Confederacy,
lays blame for violent bigot rally on
"very, very violent alt-left."

"Those who will not reason are bigots, those
who cannot are fools, and those who dare not
are slaves."
                              - George Gordon Byron

Aug. 16th. Fallout from Trump remarks equating Neo-Nazis with those protesting Neo-Nazis sees condemnation from military, mass exodus of CEOs from advisory council.

"Those who never retract their opinions love themselves more than they love the truth."

– Joseph Joubert

"When you are the problem, it's hard to see it."
— Marty Rubin

Aug. 23rd- Rallying his base in Az., Trump claims
that the media are "trying to take away our
history, our heritage", hints at pardoning Arpaio,
lies about cameras being turned off before
rally's end, threatens government shutdown.

"These are the days of second-hand fantasies
and antiquated hysteria."   - Thomas Ligotti

Aug. 24th - While CEOs, arts council members defect and resign from Trump committees, evangelicals stand by their man.

CHRIST? NEVER HEARD OF HIM. I'M JUST HERE FOR THE CONFEDERATE FLAGS AND TINY HANDS.

JDUQUETTE 2017

" And what sort of lives do these people, who pose as being moral, lead themselves?"
— Oscar Wilde

Sept. 6th - Donald Trump Jr. to be interviewed by Senate Judiciary Committee tomorrow.

JDUQUETTE

"He knew that all hazards and perils were now drawing together to a point: the next day would be a day of doom, the final effort or disaster, the last gasp."
— J·R·R· Tolkien

Sept. 15th – Trump demands ESPN "Apologize for untruth" after journalist calls him "white supremacist"

HOW DARE YOU!

GHAZALA KHAN
MUSLIM BAN
LAZINESS IS A
"TRAIT IN BLACKS"
JUDGE GONZALO CURIEL
"MANY FINE PEOPLE"
1973 HOUSING BIAS SUIT
ARPAIO PARDON
CENTRAL PARK FIVE
BIRTHERISM

JOUQUETTE

"For she had eyes and chose me."
– William Shakespeare

Sept. 20th - Chief of Staff Kelly reacts to Trump's pugnacious UN speech.

BABYSITTING IS THE PITS.

J.DUQUETTE

"You become responsible, forever, for what you have tamed."
— Antoine de Saint-Exupéry

Sept. 23rd - Trump uses Ala. stump speech to call NFL players protesting racial injustice "sons of bitches", says they should be fired.

"A bigot is a stone-deaf orator."
                    - Khalil Gibran

Sept. 26ᵗʰ – After 24 tweets in 4 days, Trump claims he's "not preoccupied" with the NFL.

"We lead our lives so poorly because we arrive in the present always unprepared, incapable, and too distracted for everything." – Rainer Maria Rilke

Oct. 2ⁿᵈ –

"Those who lack the courage will always find a philosophy to justify it." – Albert Camus

Oct. 7ᵗʰ – Tillerson's days appear numbered after allegedly calling Trump a "moron".

"On some great and glorious day, the plain folks of the land will reach their heart's desire at last and the White House will be adorned by a downright moron." – H.L. Mencken

Oct. 10ᵗʰ – Trump once again boasts of his I.Q., suggests he and Tillerson should compare results.

"People who boast of their I.Q. are losers." – Stephen Hawking

Oct. 12th - WH adviser Conway congratulates president on "his practice of elevating and empowering women."

"Delusions, carefully implanted, are difficult to correct."

– Joost A.M. Meerloo

Oct. 13th - Trump says he met with "the president of the Virgin Islands", seemingly unaware that he is, in fact, their President.

KNOWING YOUR JOB IS SO FAKE NEWS

SOUQUETTE

"In a hierarchy, every employee tends to rise to his level of incompetence."
— Laurence J. Peter

Oct. 15th. Woman who claims Trump groped her subpoenas campaign for all documents relating to multiple assault allegations.

"Here is a man whose life and actions the world has already condemned — yet whose enormous fortune has already brought him acquittal!"

— Marcus Tullius Cicero

Oct. 17th — Trump lashes out at McCain for warning of "half-baked nationalism" with threat to "be careful because at some point I fight back."

WHEN THE GOING GETS TOUGH, THE TOUGH GET BONE SPURS

"Bullies are just men who don't know they are cowards, of course."
— Antonia Hodgson

Oct. 19th - Trump grades himself a "10" on Puerto Rico response while one-third of the island doesn't have drinkable water, 80% are still without power.

"Perfect confidence is granted to the less talented as a consolation prize."   - Robert Hughes

Oct. 19th - Trump fails to make good on promise of $25K check to soldier's family until Washington Post reports on it.

"I say, that power must never be trusted without a check."
— John Adams

"Who knows himself a braggart, let him fear this,
for it will come to pass that every braggart shall
be found an ass."
　　　　　　　　　　　　　　- William Shakespeare

Oct. 27th - White House affirms position that the 16-plus women accusing Trump of sexual harassment are lying.

"The truth does not change according to our ability to stomach it." — Flannery O'Connor

Oct. 28th - Federal grand jury approves first criminal charges in Mueller's investigation of Trump campaign.

"Everything has to come to an end, sometime."
- L. Frank Baum

Nov. 3rd - Responding to questions around State Dept. vacancies, Trump says he's "the only one that matters."

"The only crime is pride." - Sophocles

NOV. 11th -

"I like people who weren't captured."
— Donald J. Trump

"The liar was the hottest to defend his veracity, the coward his courage, the ill-bred his gentlemanliness, and the cad his honor."

— Margaret Mitchell

Nov. 21st - Trump offers support for Moore because accused child molester running for Senate "totally denies" allegations.

ALWAYS HAPPY TO SUPPORT "VERY FINE PEOPLE" WHERE I SEE 'EM! NOW... LET'S HIT THE MALL!

BRING THE GRANDKIDS?

J DUQUETTE

"Find out who you are and do it on purpose."
    - Dolly Parton

Nov. 25th - Time Magazine says there's "not a speck of truth" to Trump's claims he "passed" on "probably" being named "Person of the Year."

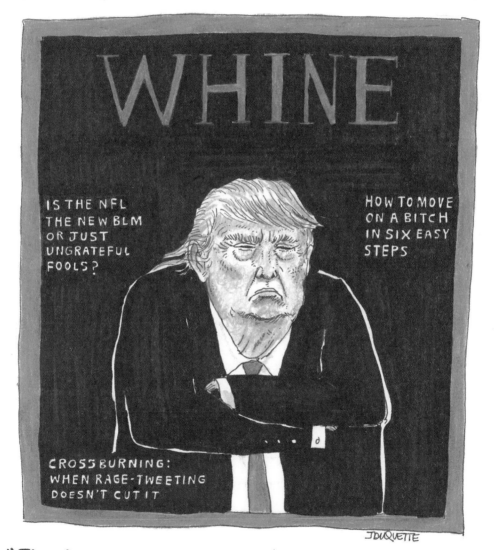

"The fact I'm not transfixed in front of the nearest mirror takes a great deal of self-control."
— Anne Rice

Nov. 27th - Trump claims his Access Hollywood "pussy grabbing" video is fake.

"I said it, I was wrong, and I apologize."
— Donald J. Trump

Nov. 27th - Trump makes "Pocahontas" joke about Sen. Warren during event honoring Navajo code talkers.

"I don't mind making jokes, but I don't want to look like one."
— Marilyn Monroe

Dec. 2nd- Trump tweets that he "had to fire Flynn because he lied to the FBI," essentially admitting to obstruction of justice.

TWEET, DON'T FAIL ME NOW.

"A storyteller makes up things to help other people; a liar makes up things to help himself."
— Daniel Wallace

Dec. 4th - Trump announces he will remove more than 2 million acres of protected territory from two Utah national monuments.

"Only a dummy would give this up for something as common as money. Are you a dummy?"
— Roald Dahl

Dec. 6th - Trump Jr. cites "attorney-client privilege", refuses to tell lawmakers what he and father discussed about Trump Tower meeting with Russians.

"But ignorance is no reason with a fool for holding his tongue."   - George MacDonald

Dec. 9th - At rally backing accused child
molester, Trump reiterates false claim that
he won 2016 election "by a landslide."

"The older I get, the more clearly I remember
things that never happened." — Mark Twain

Dec. 11th - Press Sec'y Sanders accuses media of intentionally putting out false information.

INTENTIONALLY FAKE NEWS! LIKE, SAYING OBAMA WAS BORN IN KENYA. OR, THAT 3-5 MILLION ILLEGALS VOTED IN THE 2016 ELECTION. OR THAT THE "ACCESS HOLLYWOOD" TAPE IS FAKE. OR THAT YOU SENT CONDOLENCE LETTERS TO WAR WIDOWS WHEN YOU DIDN'T. OR SAYING MEXICO IS GOING TO PAY FOR YOUR WALL. OR THAT GLOBAL WARMING IS A CHINESE HOAX. OR THAT OBAMA HAD YOUR "WIRES TAPPED." OR THAT YOU SAW THOUSANDS OF MUSLIMS CHEERING IN NEW JERSEY ON 9/11... OR... OR... OR... OR... OR... OR... OR...

"The trouble with her is that she lacks the power of conversation but not the power of speech."
                                        - George Bernard Shaw

"He had his choice, and he liked the worst."
— John Ciardi

Dec. 23rd - Trump reportedly rages over immigration, says Haitians "all have AIDS" and Nigerians live in "huts?"

"I'll bet my autopsy reveals my mouth is too big."
— Bill Watterson

Dec. 28th. Trump tweets that the U.S. "could use a little bit of that good old Global Warming" to cope with record snowfall.

"Ignorance is relatively easy to overcome; stupidity is much harder." — Marty Rubin

Dec. 29th - Trump gives wide-ranging New York Times interview riddled with lies, fake grammar, and baseless bragging.

"The greatest enemy of knowledge is not ignorance, it is the illusion of knowledge." - Daniel J. Boorstin

4

IN WHICH SERVILITY TRUMPS STABILITY

Jan. 2nd - Trump tweets that his "nuclear button is much bigger and more powerful" than North Korea's.

IF THEY DIDN'T WANT ME TO PLAY WITH IT THEY SHOULDN'T HAVE MADE IT SO SHINY

" Mary wished to say something very sensible, but knew not how."
— Jane Austen

Jan. 3rd - Bannon calls Trump Jr. meeting with Russians "treasonous", Trump responds by saying Bannon has "lost his mind".

"Later the brothers had quarrelled, one of those family quarrels we all know with deeply entangled roots, impossible to cure because neither side speaks clearly, each having much to hide."
— Giuseppe Tomasi di Lampedusa

Jan. 6th. Trump pushes back on mental fitness questions, tweets he is "like, really smart" and a "stable genius."

PFFFF!
THIS IS SO EASY,
EVEN ERIC COULD DO IT!
I CAN NAME ALMOST
EVERY COLOR ON THIS
BRAIN BOX THING!

JDURVETTE

"He has never been known to use a word that might send a reader to the dictionary."
— William Faulkner

Jan 7th - Amidst growing concerns around Trump's fitness for office, GOP leaders stand by their man.

"By their passive acceptance, these populations become accessories to whatever is done in their name."

— Frank Herbert

Jan. 9th. Bannon steps down from Breitbart News.

"Doffing the ego's safe glory, he finds his
naked reality."
— Dag Hammarskjöld

Jan. 10th - Trump offers no commitment to interview with Mueller, incorrectly claims "everyone agrees there's no collusion?"

MAYBE IF I CLICK MY HEELS AND SAY "NO COLLUSION" A BAZILLION TIMES, THEY'LL GIVE ME ONE OF THOSE FLYING MONKEYS SO I CAN HITCH A RIDE BACK TO MOSCOW AND GET BACK TO HITTING ON RUSSIAN MODELS.

JDUQUETTE

"A man that flies from his fear may find that he has only taken a short cut to meet it."
— J.R.R. Tolkien

Jan. 11th - Frustrated Trump lashes out at immigrants from "shithole countries"?

HOW'S THIS FOR A "BILL OF LOVE"?

JDUQUETTE

"National hatred is something peculiar. You always find it strongest and most violent where there is the lowest degree of culture."
-Johann Wolfgang von Goethe

"Tolerance of intolerance is cowardice."
— Ayaan Hirsi Ali

Jan. 15th.

"One day we will learn that the heart can never be totally right when the head is totally wrong."

— Martin Luther King, Jr.

Jan. 17th - 9 Park Service board members quit, citing concerns with Trump administration's priorities regarding national parks.

"Be with a leader when he is right, stay with him when he is still right, but leave him when he is wrong."

- Abraham Lincoln

Jan. 20th - Thousands take to the streets in protest on the one-year anniversary of the women's march.

"Remember all men would be tyrants if they could. If particular care and attention is not paid to the Ladies, we are determined to foment a rebellion and will not hold ourselves bound by any laws in which we have no voice or representation."
    -Abigail Adams

Jan. 21st - White House releases images of
Trump sitting at an empty desk and staring
into space as proof he's "working" during
gov't. shutdown.

"Pretending is one of our greatest
pleasures. But you have to know you're pretending."
— Marty Rubin

Jan. 23rd - AG Sessions interviewed by Mueller as part of Russia probe.

"I think your deputies are in trouble."
— Brian Cook

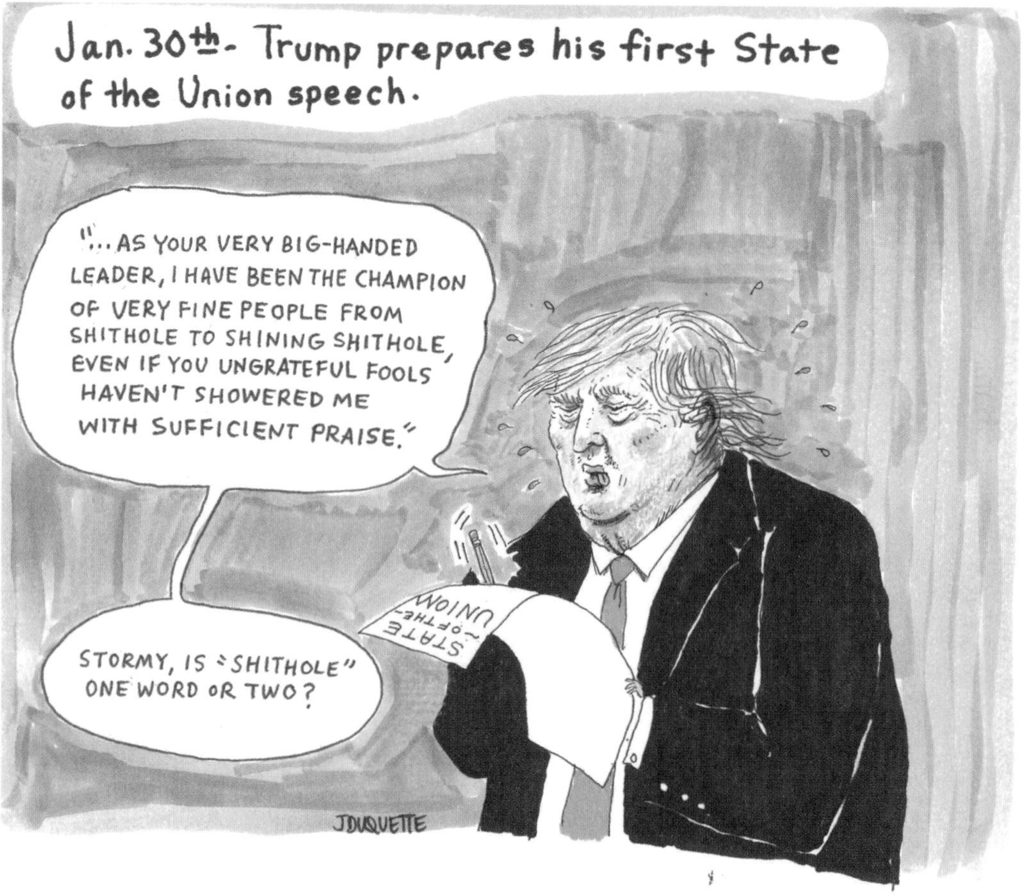

"He had nothing to say and he said it."
-Ambrose Bierce

Feb. 1ˢᵗ - Forever obsessed with crowd sizes,
Trump tweets lie that his SOTU address had
the "highest number in history" viewing.

"Belief is a wonderful way to pass the time until
the facts come in."   - Carl R. White

Feb. 1st - Russian spy chief visited D.C. despite being on U.S. "blacklist"; interestingly timed with deadline for Russian sanctions.

"One hand washes the other." - Seneca

Feb. 6th. Trump tells Pentagon to organize a grand military parade.

"War hath no fury like a non-combatant."
—Charles Edward Montague

Feb. 10th - Eric Trump tweets teaser pic of new "Trump" magazine following 2009's failed publishing venture.

NO BIG WORDS!
LOTS OF DRAWINGS!

Trump

THE HACKY MAG FROM A TACKY WAG

IN THIS ISSUE:
THE UNSUNG HEROES
BEING ACCUSED OF
"DOMESTIC ABUSE"
BY A BUNCH OF FIVES

DIY GRAVEYARD-SIZED CLOSETS TO HIDE
ALL THOSE PESKY SKELETONS (AND FBI-PROOF, TO BOOT!)

GROVELLING IN RUSSIAN: 5 SIMPLE PHRASES

COPING WITH LARGE HAND SYNDROME

DADDY-DAUGHTER VALENTINE'S DAY IDEAS

ALL PROCEEDS
GO TO THE
TRUMP LEGAL
DEFENSE FUND

JOULVETTE

"...The stupid person's idea of a clever person."
-Elizabeth Bowen

Feb. 19th. Trump returns to golf course after taking a "respectful" two days off following school shooting.

"Jesus! Where will it end? How low do you have to stoop in this country to be President?"
— Hunter S. Thompson

Feb. 21st - Trump holds "listening session" for Americans impacted by school gun violence, armed with reminder to listen.

"Men more frequently require to be reminded than informed."
— Samuel Johnson

Feb. 22nd – U.S. Citizenship & Immigration Services removing phrase "nation of immigrants" from its mission statement.

SOUNDS GOOD, THE DOOR'S THAT WAY.

JDUQUETTE

"No man can occupy the office of President without realizing that he is President of all the people." — Franklin D. Roosevelt

Feb. 23rd - Trump pushes for arming teachers, says schools shouldn't be "gun-free zones" in response to mass shooting epidemic.

"The less he understands something, the more firmly he believes in it."   — Wilhelm Reich

Feb. 27th. Kushner's security clearance is downgraded, preventing him from accessing top-secret intelligence.

"I am not fit for this office and never should have been here."   — Warren G. Harding

"I have a lot of experience with people smarter than I am."   - Gerald R. Ford

Mar. 10th - Bannon takes garbage message
to France, tells far-right National Front
party ⁼ Let them call you racist... wear it as
a badge of honor"

HYGIENE WILL
NOT REPLACE US!
HYGIENE WILL
NOT REPLACE US!

J DUQUETTE

"It matters, it always matters, to name rubbish
as rubbish... to do otherwise is to legitimize it."
- Salman Rushdie

Mar. 16th - Trump's budget proposal requests $639B for defense, wipes out funding for Meals on Wheels, Nat'l Endowment for the Arts, PBS.

"I hope that something better comes along."
~ Jim Henson

March 29ᵗʰ - Trump being advised that he doesn't need Chief of Staff or Communications Director.

"Authority without wisdom is like a heavy axe
without an edge, fitter to bruise than polish."
— Anne Bradstreet

April 3rd —

"If you do not tell the truth about yourself,
you cannot tell it about other people."
                                    —Virginia Woolf

April 3rd - In series of tweets, Trump panders to his base's fear of immigrants, says "our country is being stolen"

"...Remember you are not dealing with creatures of logic, but with creatures bristling with prejudice and motivated by pride and vanity."
— Dale Carnegie

April 5th - Trump breaks silence over Stormy Daniels, says he didn't know about lawyer's $130K payment to porn star.

"Everyone listened to this amusing narrative with great interest, and the moment Behemoth concluded it, they all shouted in unison: 'Lies!'"
                                                        - Mikhail Bulgakov

"Those who can make you believe absurdities can make you commit atrocities." — Voltaire

April 29th -

"A person reveals his character by nothing so clearly as the joke he resents."

— Georg Christoph Lichtenburg

May 1st - Mueller's list of questions for Trump leaked.

1. **WHAT KIND OF GOVERNMENT DOES THE U·S· HAVE?**
   - A.) CONSTITUTIONAL REPUBLIC
   - B.) SUPERSIZE WITH FRIES
   - C.) PASS

2. **FINISH THIS SENTENCE : "2.8 MILLION IS..."**
   - A.) A STAGGERINGLY EMBARASSING AMOUNT TO LOSE THE POPULAR VOTE BY.
   - B.) THE NUMBER OF TREMENDOUS RUSSIAN BOTS WHO ARE WORKING DUTIFULLY ON TRUMP'S BEHALF.
   - C.) I'M PRETTY SURE THAT'S NOT A NUMBER.

3. **WHAT IS THE BIGGEST THREAT TO OUR DEMOCRACY?**
   - A.) THE INTENTIONAL, TARGETED SPREAD OF MISINFORMATION BY FOREIGN ACTORS.
   - B.) A COMEDIAN TELLING JOKES THAT HURT MY FEELINGS.
   - C.) ANDERSON COOPER. OH, AND BROWN PEOPLE.

THESE BIG WORDS ARE A DISGRACE!

JOUSUETTE

"Oh my soul, be prepared for the coming of the Stranger. Be prepared for him who knows how to ask questions."
— T·S· Eliot

May 7th - Giuliani, defending Trump's lies and shifting story on Stormy Daniels hush money payment, says = "I don't know how you separate fact and opinion."

"We had no domestic attacks under Bush."
— Rudy Giuliani

"The history of mankind from the very beginning has been a history of over-trusted trustees, corrupted by their unchecked opportunities."
– H.G. Wells

May 24th _ Trump says NFL players who kneel during national anthem =shouldn't be in the country ?

May 27th - Poll shows half of Republicans believe Trump's lies that "millions of illegals" voted in 2016 election.

"**Faith, n.** Belief without evidence in what is told by one who speaks without knowledge, of things without parallel." — Ambrose Bierce

May 30th - Roseanne blames sleeping pills for racist tweets.

"The sleepy like to make excuses."
— Benedict of Nursia

June 3rd - Trump's lawyers change story, now say he "dictated" statement on Trump Tower meeting.

HEY, I JUST GIVE THE VERY BEST INFORMATION POSSIBLE AT THE TIME.

JDUQUETTE

"He certainly didn't dictate."

- Sarah Huckabee Sanders

"The idea of America is a mutt-culture, isn't it?
Who the hell is America if not everybody else?
We are—and should be—a big, messy, anarchistic
polyglot of dialects and accents and different
skin tones."
                                    —Anthony Bourdain

June 10th-

" What greater thing is there for two human souls than to feel that they are joined to strengthen each other, to be at one with each other in silent unspeakable memories."
— George Eliot

June 12th - Trump compliments Kim Jong Un as "funny", "talented", says he "loves his people".

"You are truly home only when you find your tribe."
— Srividya Srinivasan

5

A CONFEDERACY OF PUTZES
CLOSES OUT YEAR TWO

"All cruelty springs from weakness."
  - Seneca

June 21st -

"You'd be surprised how expensive it costs to look this cheap." - Dolly Parton

June 26th. Supreme Court upholds Trump's bigoted Muslim ban.

WELL, SHUCKS— LET'S BE CIVIL ENOUGH SO I CAN EAT A STEAK IN PEACE, AM I RIGHT?

"I never wonder to see men wicked, but I often wonder to see them not ashamed."
—Jonathan Swift

"We can draw lessons from the past, but we cannot live in it."
— Lyndon B. Johnson

July 9th - Trump visits the UK.

NOT ENOUGH
HOT AIR.

JDUQUETTE

"We don't want other countries laughing at us
anymore. And they won't be. They won't be."
                                    - Donald J. Trump

July 17th.

"THERE WASN'T NO COLLUSION"

"He that is good for making excuses is seldom good for anything else."

-Benjamin Franklin

July 29th - Trump again tweets false claim
that his poll numbers are higher than Lincoln's.

"All I know is what's on the internet."
— Donald J. Trump

Aug·18th·

Aug. 21<u>st</u>.

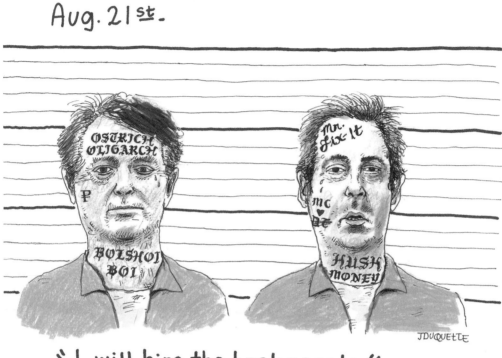

Aug. 23rd – National Enquirer boss who helped "kill" damaging Trump stories leading up to election granted immunity in hush money probe.

"But it is always the facts that will not fit in that are significant." –Agatha Christie

Aug. 28th. Trump claims Google search results are "rigged" against him.

"Stories of imagination tend to upset those without one." — Terry Pratchett

Aug. 31st - Another day, another person in Trump's orbit implicated, indicted, or pleading guilty in Mueller probe.

"The witch was too much afraid..."
- L. Frank Baum

Sept. 5th.

"In a time of deceit, telling the truth is a
revolutionary act."   - George Orwell

Sept. 7th -

"The slickest way in the world to lie is to tell the right amount of truth at the right time — and then shut up." - Robert A. Heinlein

"40 Wall Street... was the tallest. And then, when they built the World Trade Center, it became known as the second-tallest. And now, it's the tallest."
— Donald J. Trump 9-11-01

Sept. 17th -

"You've got to deny, deny, deny, and push back on these women. If you admit to anything and any culpability, then you're dead."
— Donald J. Trump

Sept. 21st - Trump promises more firings at the FBI and DOJ to get rid of "lingering stench."

"You can dress up greed, but you can't stop the stench."   - Craig D. Lounsbrough

Sept. 27th.

SCARING THE SHIT OUT OF MEN
WHO DESERVE TO BE SCARED
DURING THIS "SCARY TIME FOR
YOUNG MEN IN AMERICA."

"Merrick fucking Garland."

— Jesse Duquette

"We need a President who isn't a laughing stock to the entire world."
                              - Donald J. Trump

"Finish, good lady; the bright day is done,
And we are for the Dark." -William Shakespeare

Oct. 15 th. Trump hangs painting in WH of himself with former GOP presidents.

"Paintings. Or the collapse of time in images."
- Paul Auster

Oct. 24th. Bombs sent to Clintons, Obamas, CNN, ex-AG, and others.

"Fathers, do not provoke your children to anger."
— Ephesians 6:4

Oct. 25th.

"We'll see what happens."
- Donald J. Trump

Oct. 26th.

"My supporters are the smartest, strongest, most hard working and most loyal that we have seen in our countries (sic) history."
— Donald J. Trump

Oct. 30<u>th</u>.

"We the people are the rightful masters of both Congress and the courts, not to overthrow the Constitution but to overthrow the men who pervert the Constitution." — Abraham Lincoln

Nov. 2nd.

"Choose well. Your choice is brief, and yet endless." — Johann Wolfgang von Goethe

Nov. 4th. Trump claims Abrams "isn't qualified" to be Georgia's governor.

- GRADUATED MAGNA CUM LAUDE WITH BA IN INTERDISCIPLINARY STUDIES
- EARNED MASTER OF PUBLIC AFFAIRS DEGREE FROM UNIVERSITY OF TEXAS
- EARNED JURIS DOCTOR FROM YALE LAW SCHOOL
- CO-FOUNDED SUCCESSFUL BUSINESS THAT DIDN'T GO BANKRUPT
- APPOINTED DEPUTY CITY ATTORNEY FOR ATLANTA AT AGE 29
- MEMBER OF GA. GENERAL ASSEMBLY FROM 2007–2017
- LIFETIME MEMBER OF COUNCIL ON FOREIGN RELATIONS

- CAN FIND NAMBIA ON A MAP.
- FAKE-FIRED CELEBRITIES ON A REALITY TV SHOW
- KNOWS THE FIRST 3 WORDS TO THE STAR-SPANGLED BANNER
- HAS "THE BEST WORDS"

"Nobody asked _your_ opinion, said Alice."
— Lewis Carroll

Nov. 7th- Trump ousts Sessions.

Nov. 12th.

"I knew he didn't love me, but I adored him anyway."
— Patti Smith

Nov. 14th.

"If you buy a box of cereal you have to have voter ID." — Donald J. Trump

Nov. 15th – # CEREAL PICKS
FOR
SERIAL PRICKS

FROSTED FAKES

HONEYCOMBOVER

SHOULD'VE BEEN "MUSLIM BRAN"

RACIST BRAN

CREAM OF DECEIT

I EAT MY CEREAL WITH A FORK!

HONEY BUNCHES OF UNQUALIFIED OATS

FOLDING GRAHAMS

JOUQUETTE

" I don't believe in climate change."
— Donald J. Trump

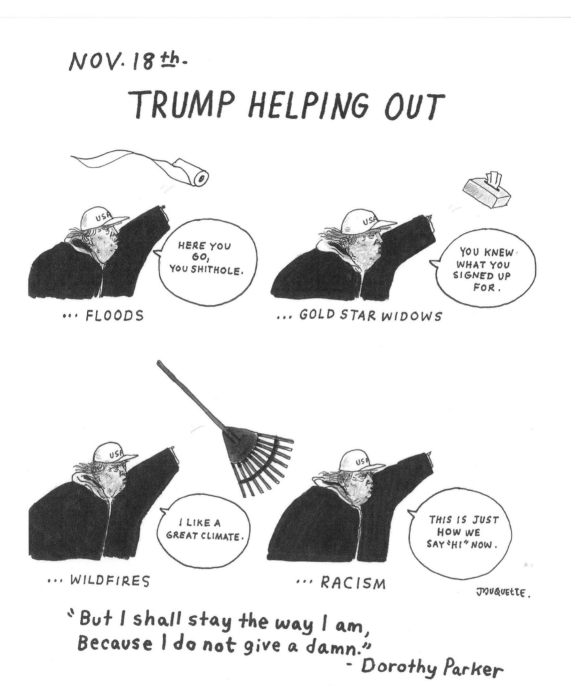

"We all romanticize the people we adore."
- John Green

Nov. 29th.

IT'S ALMOST AS IF AN UNREPENTANT CROOK CAN'T DO HIS CRIMES WITHOUT BEING HELD ACCOUNTABLE, WHAT— EVER THAT MEANS.

JDUQUETTE

"You can't run away from trouble. There ain't no place that far." - Joel Chandler Harris

Dec. 22nd.

"A shutdown falls on the president's lack of leadership. He can't even control his party and get people together in a room. A shutdown means the president is weak." — Donald J. Trump

Dec. 31st.

"Folks, it's time to evolve. We're supposed to keep evolving. Evolution did not end with us growing opposable thumbs. You do know that, right?" – Bill Hicks

"To permit irresponsible authority is to sell disaster."

—Robert A. Heinlein